D0206191

JOHANN SEBASTIAN BACH

Johann Sebastian Bach

Heritage and Obligation

BY PAUL HINDEMITH

NEW HAVEN: YALE UNIVERSITY PRESS

First published, November 1952
Second printing, August 1959

JOHANN SEBASTIAN BACH

*A speech delivered on
September 12, 1950 at the
Bach commemoration of the
city of Hamburg, Germany*

POSTSCRIPT OF BACH'S LETTER TO J. E. BACH

P.M. Ohnerachtet der Herr Vetter sich geneigt offerieren, fernerhin mit dergleichen liqueur zu assistiren; So muss doch wegen übermässiger hiesigen Abgaben es depreciren. Denn da die Fracht 16 gr. der Überbringer 2 gr. der Visitator 2 gr. die Landaccise 5 gr. 3 pfg. u. general accise 3 gr. gekostet hat, als können der Herr Vetter selbsten ermessen, dass mir jedes Maass fast 5 gr. zu stehen kömmt, welches denn vor ein Geschencke alzu kostbar ist.

I

Bavarian Franconia had produced excellent wine in 1748. Cantor Johann Elias Bach of Schweinfurt, wishing to please his cousin Sebastian with whom he had studied, sent a cask of his product to Leipzig, to his cousin, his cousin's wife, and their children, whom he had tutored. A letter of acknowledgment came from Leipzig, but the postscript must have caused Elias some wonder: the Bach family "deprecated" his well-meant plan to "assist further with such liqueur." Somehow the cask had lost part of its contents on the way, and the recipient had been charged the fees for freight and customs so that "the price per quart," as the letter says, "came to almost five groschen, which is certainly too much for a gift."

I have often wondered whether, in the bicentenary year of countless Bach addresses, which were undoubtedly as well intended as cousin Elias' gift, their celebrated subject would not have repudiated them too, somewhat grumblingly, in his Saxon dialect. Very likely it would have offended his highly developed sense of proportion to see the two words "Bach and ——" followed by every variety of noun, linking him to all imaginable things in heaven and earth.

Or would he have outgrown wonder? What stranger thing could happen to him than to be designated, in the 1930's, an antireligious composer and as such one of the cultural pillars of Brown Germany, or most recently, with the assistance of Communist China's minister of culture, a forerunner of Red internationalism? In the two hundred years since his death each rising generation has seen him differently; his creations have been analyzed and criticized, performed and deformed, used and abused; books and pamphlets, paintings and plaster busts have made him a common household article; in short he has finally been transformed into a statue. It seems to me that having this statue constantly before our eyes has impaired our view of the true stature of Bach, both of the man and of his work. Even his most genuine and significant monument, the still unsurpassed complete edition of his compositions published by the Bachgesellschaft, does its share to cloud our view of him. In it the grave stands beside the gay, the ponderous beside the slight, looking equally impressive; the arduously conceived work and the facile quasi-

8

improvisation are neighbors. True, the real values have become known to expert and layman alike; the greater creations have come to be distinguished from the less perfect. But the most important factor in evaluation, that which makes the works of masters like Beethoven and Wagner so translucent—the knowledge of these composers' own attitude toward each of their creations—is entirely absent in the collected works, the *Gesamtausgabe*. Its author had a clam-like reticence toward his work; many things that might have permitted us a clearer appraisal have been lost; and finally, at the time the complete edition appeared the technique of editing music was not so developed as it is now. Today a monumental work of this sort could and should be published in a more perfect form, making the composer's idea plain to every reader and user by placing opposite each printed page a photographic reproduction of the manuscript it was set from. Only under these conditions would the character of the script, the recognizable tempo of the writing, and other signs visible in the notation reveal the attitude and intent of the composer toward his opus at the time he was writing.

9

Other editions of Bach's works, including all the arrangements for instrumental and vocal combinations not originally called for, are even less adapted to show the real Bach than are the *Gesamtausgabe*. Incredible things have been published in the guise of serving practical demands. From outright falsifications to well-intended suggestions about fingerings and bowings, all served up and received as eternal truths, there is every degree of tampering by little men with the work of one of the greatest.

Furthermore, what we get from biographies of Bach too readily fosters our inclination to take the statue for the living being. The earliest biographical notes, dating from shortly after his death, are so fragmentary that a mythical being is suggested. Later he is described as a martyr sacrificing himself for his art; as a knight of chivalry fighting against all comers, since the world of his contemporaries cannot comprehend his greatness and impedes his mission wherever possible; as an upright citizen without fear or falsehood; as an all-embracing being who not only performs daily miracles in his art but knows the directest access to the universe and is an intimate friend of the *Creator Spiritus*.

Thus he became that banal figure which meets our eyes every day: a man in a full-skirted coat, with a wig he never lays by. If circumstances permit artificial figures thus to assume the significance of living beings, we ourselves should beware of becoming the victims of this transformation. Admittedly our master has done much to induce this misconstruction. About his human qualities his musical works are quite naturally a poor source of information. And of the immediate human testimony—some seventy letters known to be written by him—the larger part are ratings and recommendations of students or deal with matters that hardly seem to merit the attention of a great spirit. Only a tenth of the letters are of a more personal nature, but these, strangely enough, are even more misleading and disappointing for those seeking extraordinary human and artistic revelations.

The research of recent decades has in many respects showed how in Bach's case towering artistic eminence and personal indistinctness, superhuman intuition and pettiness are mingled. The mythical being is beginning slowly to change back into a human being, the glittering hero is growing into a lovable fellow citizen notwithstanding all his failings, the statue of stone and bronze is becoming flesh and blood. Now we see a man who, in spite of a life spent in petit bourgeois doings and surroundings, has built up a completely independent world of artistic creation. The trivialities of his daily routine apart from composition he seems to discharge with a kind of self-torturing insistence. He apparently lives in harmony with his family, although domestic happiness is not abundant. His first wife dies after thirteen years of married life. Eleven of his children die either at birth or in early childhood. Of the nine remaining children five will become musicians. One of them, highly recommended by his father for an organist's position, goes into debt, leads an evil life, has to run away, and dies soon after. To the other four with their entirely different sort of musicianship their father must seem an enigmatic and possibly useless vestige of a past epoch, as do those composers today who write with conviction in the style of Wagner. One of the sons bluntly labels him an "old peruke." These sons are certainly no models of filial love, as witness the eagerness with which they grab their father's heritage, and their leaving his widow, their mother or their stepmother, to penury, so that she finally dies a charity case and goes to a pauper's grave. Another son is feebleminded; of the four daughters only one marries, the other three die old maids. Bach himself is a tolerant and hospitable man, not averse to the little amenities of life. A good provider, he is out to do well for himself, especially in the matter of financial advantage. As is so often found with men who work in the arts and sciences with the most comprehensive wisdom but in their daily life dwell in pettiness, he likes to wrangle over minor matters, especially when he feels himself unjustly treated, which he does rather frequently. He argues vehemently, in endless letters to his superiors, on behalf of his opinions. If one reads the statements of the opposite party, the abysmal turpitude of the surrounding world is not absolutely proved. They charge him with various irregularities, even with carelessness in the performance of his duties, which in view of the strict sense of artistic responsibility evident in his compositions is hard to understand. Sometimes he must have been rather malevolent, or else the duke of Weimar, his employer, who was by no means hostile to him, would not

have imprisoned him for one month in 1717.
The protocol reads: "November 6 the erst-
while concertmaster and organist Bach was ar-
rested because of his stubbornness in claiming
his release from service; December 2 he was
set at liberty with notice of dishonorable dis-
missal."

Not only Bach the man but also Bach the
musician may, after the above statements, lose
some of his fairy-tale glitter and marble-statue
pomposity. More or less everyone thinks of
him as abiding in an almost continual droning
of organ sounds, which toward the end of his
life swelled into perpetual harmonious rever-
berations. But the fact is that in Bach's time organs were different; the resounding organ that
imitates a full orchestra did not exist. The tone
of the organ, although colorful, was thin and
somewhat shrill, without those syrupy addi-
tions which seem to many of our modern lis-
teners typical of the instrument. During the
last thirty-three years of his life—or half of it
—Bach was no longer employed as organist.
Although he may have played the organ frequently even then, he preferred the harpsichord. On those few occasions which added so
immensely to his glory as a performer, like the

uncontested contest with Marchand and the visit to Frederick the Great in Potsdam, Bach played the harpsichord, not the organ.

As a choir director he appears no less impressive to us, inspiring his Thomas Church choristers to powerful vocal manifestations. But the impression cannot have been too powerful, for a choir of only about sixteen boys' and adolescents' voices was available for each Sunday's cantata, accompanied by a still smaller orchestra. To be sure the complete choir of the school, when sickness did not take its toll, consisted of fifty to sixty singers, but they had to be apportioned to four different church services. When they sang all together, as at the annual performance of the Passion, neither of the two choruses in the St. Matthew Passion, for example, could have had more than twenty-five to twenty-eight singers. This seems poor compared with the "normal" size of choirs and orchestras of Bach performances in our time, which do their drills with the overwhelming power and precision of companies of infantry, led by a commander for whose sole glorification often enough the entire show seems to be arranged. One is always inclined to interpret the small number of participants in Bach's time and the limitations in sound and technique of the instruments then in use as factors hampering a composer's imagination. He would have delighted to use great choirs, so one believes, if only they had been available; Beethoven's and Wagner's orchestras would have been his ideal, and he would have discarded the chirping harpsichord in favor of a modern Steinway. Nothing supports this opinion. If one is not persuaded that only small groups of performers can convincingly show the lucidity of Bach's polyphonic choral style —entirely contrary to the choral technique of Handel, who counted on the large English choir—one needs but to study carefully the orchestral scores of the four Overtures (Suites) and the six Brandenburg Concertos. Here it is a particular pleasure to see how the composer enjoys handling the minute differences in the balance of sound in these small instrumental ensembles, a balance so sensitive that often the mere doubling of a line through several additional instruments ruins its subtle texture as much as would a doubling of the soprano line in Pamina's aria by a women's chorus. We can be sure that Bach was thoroughly content with the means of expression at hand in voices and

16

1. Die St. Thomas Kirche, 2. Die Thomas Schule
3. Der Steinerne Wasser=Kasten

Krügner Sc Lipsiæ.

THE THOMAS CHURCH AND THOMAS SCHOOL IN BACH'S TIME

instruments, and if we want to perform his music according to his intentions we ought to restore the conditions of performance of that time. Using the harpsichord as continuo instrument would not be the only step in this direction. Other kinds of strings would have to be used on our stringed instruments. The wind instruments must be built like their predecessors in size and sound. Even the distinction between choral pitch and chamber pitch should be restored.

Having got to know Bach the man and Bach the practical musician, we must turn to his activity as a teacher, his ability to preserve and develop the tradition of musical theory—again with a somewhat sober look, so as to avoid enthusiastically devising a figure unlike the original. As a teacher he apparently worked with all the advantages and handicaps of an impulsive artist bursting with music, who opens to the student an uninhibited view into the realm of musical inspiration and lets him participate in the process of creation, but who also feels the creative impatience of the genius frustrate the perseverance indispensable in all education. More often than not playing and listening on the spur of the moment seems to have replaced doctrinal instruction. (We experience all this frequently enough even with composer-teachers of much smaller stature.) And in his daily choral practice with the Thomas boys too the artist seems to have prevailed over the teacher, if we are to believe the Leipzig documents. One has the impression that in his former positions at Weimar and Cöthen, in the company of versatile musicians who needed no instruction, he felt more at home than among those youths who after all in their boyish ways were without discipline and never up to his artistic standards. The statement made in a session of the Leipzig Council shortly after his death is significant: we need for the vacant post a real cantor instead of a Kapellmeister; "Although Mr. Bach was a great musician, he was not a school man."

To the theoretical aspects of his art he shows indifference. If in style of composition he was the representative of a past era to his contemporaries, his almost exclusive devotion to questions of practical music makes him seem to us one of the first masters who in modern fashion broke away from the medieval type of musician, from those who tried to combine the well-trained man of scholarly discipline and the free-roving musical visionary. The statement must sound strange when we have grown used to seeing this very Bach as the incarnation of the academic musician nurtured on science. The basis for this is the common belief that one who writes fugues can only be a scholar. Certainly, good contrapuntal constructions demand something more than the mere emotional fancy of a naïve composer, but this is far from being science: scientific methods can never be applied to artistic creation. A similar case in more recent decades was Max Reger. Was not the halo of the musical savant, which is meaningless for the musician, attributed to him too? But if ever a musician composed unhampered by scholarly considerations and with rabid creative impetus, rabid to the point of carelessness, it was Reger. Bach's musical mind must have been similar, although we always sense in him a sober pre-eminence over any of his actions that prevents him from getting lost in nebulousness or ebbing away into platitudes.

Had an archmusician of Bach's type shown any serious interest in the scientific branch of music, its theory, it would easily have been satisfied in the eighteenth century. The pre-

cepts of the Frenchman Rameau dared over-
throw a harmonic system which had remained
unchallenged for almost five hundred years;
a straightforward man of musical practice like
Tartini in Italy searched for the universally
valid principles governing the building ma-
terials of music and their handling. In Germany too they fought eagerly for and against
the new ideas which were pressing in from out-
side. Stern theorists like Marpurg disputed
with practical musicians like Kirnberger
(whose attempt to build Bach's teaching methods posthumously into a more comprehensive
theoretical system was only moderately success-
ful); rising music journalism, at that time rep-
resented by Scheibe and Mattheson, expressed
its opinion; and so, with acute perception,
did such experts in musical craftsmanship as
Daube. Bach remained apart from this tur-
moil. To be sure, he used the newest advance
in musical science, twelve-tone equal tempera-
ment, but obviously merely as a welcome aid
in realizing his wide-ranging tonal visions. The
effective basis of his technique remains the old
thorough bass, the *Generalbass,* which can by
no means be regarded as a fundamental law
but solely as a stylistically determined regu-

lator of tone combination. It died with Bach. In a letter which Philipp Emanuel, Bach's son, wrote to Kirnberger we read: "You are entitled to make known that my musical doctrines, like those of my late father, are opposed to Rameau's."

We might say that if the Marpurgs, Rameaus, and Daubes represent one branch of musical art we shall always prefer the other, that of an artist like Bach, which is perhaps less intellectual but in its capacity to move us seems to come straight from heaven. This statement would be somewhat unfair. For one thing any musician, even the most gifted, takes a place second to Bach's at the start. The musical achievement of a Bach must necessarily overshadow what surrounds him. Secondly, even a musician of Bach's rank can realize his visions only if he finds a thoroughly organized tone system available, which is possible solely through the preliminary work of skilled theorists. All considerations of technique in composition, rules of harmony, melody, and form must be based on their findings. This being so, we must be careful not to derive any teaching system for general use from the working methods of the genius with their licence, short-

cuts, and short circuits. We cannot make a
Bach's way of learning and teaching ours without running the danger of cleverly using all his
artifice to provide shallow tone structures but
fulfilling none of the other conditions that are
valid with him and such as he.

II

The intent to speak of what we inherit from Bach and our obligation toward this inheritance I have scarcely fulfilled by stripping him of some of the tinsel glory which in the course of time has surrounded his figure. What was thus removed had not been in his personal possession, so he could not bequeath it; nor did he contribute anything to the distorting legend—although in a negative way, through silence, he has done much, as I have said, to build it up. I felt impelled to make the somewhat prosaic observations above in order to provide the proper light for a view of what I believe to be our heritage from him.

I do not use heritage in the literal sense. The literal heritage, his music proper, has conquered our souls as has hardly any other master's work. It was hidden and forgotten for a long time, like buried treasure in romantic tales, but finally several generations ago we found it again. We acquired it to possess it, "erwarben sie um sie zu besitzen," to quote *Faust*. What could be said in praise of this art and its possession could hardly do more than repeat statements made before, commonplaces and cheap enthusiasm, unless one re-

sorted to technical, historical, esthetic considerations which are of no interest to the layman. No better service can be rendered to this
art and its creator than to perform it in his
spirit, thus making ourselves always anew its
true acquirers and possessors.

The heritage I have in mind is of a more
general, more comprehensive, supramusical
kind. To understand it no detour through
hearing and absorbing Bach's music is needed
(since complete absorption of that will always
remain an unattainable goal); we need only
concern ourselves with what we know beyond
his purely artistic achievement: his attitude
toward the creative vocation. This sounds not
too significant, since everyone in his profession
faces similar problems, although on a smaller
scale. But just this common validity seems to
make Bach's attitude toward his gift from
heaven a fact which is highly instructive to all
of us. Here we can follow him with the fullest
comprehension, without considering the extraordinary in him, his musical creativeness.
Here we can inherit what will be of the most
general human usefulness.

What was his attitude?

We know he had to struggle against adverse

circumstances which a creator of the rank of Bach should have been spared: sorrow and misfortune in his family; the not too satisfactory life of lower middle-class people; unceasing quarrels with differently minded superiors; lack of recognition of his essential talents—how many human beings succumb in each generation, feeling themselves unable to cope with such adversities. But it was not only local and domestic difficulties that had to be overcome; the whole musical situation at that period would put one who did not wish to follow the general trend in a disagreeable position.

Do not let us forget that church music, Bach's main field of activity, had by no means attained that state of perfection we like to think it had: abundantly staffed, jubilating choirs we have seen did not exist, nor did thundering orchestras nor resounding organs. If Leipzig could barely support its small singing group in St. Thomas, it is easy to see what kind of mighty church music existed in smaller places. Restrictions also came from the Protestant Reformed Church, which rejected any artistic ornamentation of the service as a voluptuous digression; and the pietistic movement did its share to convince believers of the devil-

27

ish blasphemy evident in a cantata style like Bach's. Even Bach's own denomination, the orthodox Lutheran branch of the Protestant church, despite its favorable attitude toward church music suffers from obvious weaknesses if one compares its musical possibilities to those of the Roman Catholic Church—weaknesses which inevitably hamper the composer who writes for the Lutheran service.

The Roman church is the possessor of immeasurable musical wealth in the Gregorian chant. That could never be ignored; it has always served as measure and example for new religious compositions, and will probably continue to exert its regulating power upon all future musical productions for the Catholic church. Only a fraction of this treasure can be performed by the whole congregation; for the rest practiced and practicing groups of singers are required, striving for perfection in the true style of this music, a performance far removed from subjective expression and concert effectiveness. As a result of the Reformation, singing by the congregation had replaced the Gregorian chant. Although in both a religious and an educational sense it is desirable to install the singing congregation as the supporting pillar of church music, thus elevating the layman to the rank of leading artist, the immediate result must be a wearing thin of musical forms; the achievements of a well-trained group, which in daily sessions finds itself musically challenged by those complex one-voiced lines, cannot be matched by inexperienced singing groups in occasional meetings, however good their intentions. To counteract the inevitable musical attrition in the latter groups, and to make up for the limitations of their musical capacity, the introduction of an invigorating factor, concert-like performances by professional musicians, became a necessity. The choristers taking part in these depended on a constant stream of novelty which ready composers had to provide. Hasty production of this kind could avoid the danger of hollowness only if talented composers supported and directed an otherwise aimless movement. This made individual accomplishment the artistic determinant in the Protestant church, while in the Roman church even the greatest musical master could never dominate the field, since to produce anything surpassing the centuries-old liturgical inheritance was impossible. This development toward the concert in church music doubtless opened the way for Bach's cantatas and Passions as pre-eminent examples of religious music; more than that, it contributed essentially to the great rise of secular music. Yet we should ask if under those conditions really valuable church music is possible without the intervention of an extraordinary genius. The singing done by the various sects of English protestantism, in so far as they did not adopt the Roman musical ritual, seems to prove that these churches must rely on the fanaticism of an impetuous God-sent composer if their conception of church music is not to end in barrenness: English hymnody, notwithstanding its value as an emotional stimulant for the singing group, is not of high quality musically and is sometimes dangerously close to the absurd.

The situation, as we can see, was not encouraging. Certainly the church was not the place for composers seeking success. Opera was the field where glory and glamour were to be found, as the work of Keiser and Hasse shows; and at the courts of noblemen, the mansions of wealthy citizens with their less rigorous, more gracious atmosphere, an agreeably diverting art came to blossom. And one who wished by

EXAMPLES OF BACH'S MUSICAL HANDWRITING

from the Clavier-Büchlein vor Wilhelm Friedemann Bach, Library of the School of Music, Yale University

APPLICATIO. IN NOMINE IESU

CHORALE PRELUDE: WER NUR DEN LIEBEN GOTT LÄSST WALTEN

all means to remain true to religious music could have followed Handel's example and charmed the faithful with concert forms; Handel's style of oratorio composition could well have flourished in the Germany of that time. Yet Bach aimed unerringly at his single goal. He could not foresee that in the next two hundred years his compositions would come to predominate over all church music, as a result of that need of the Protestant church to rely on exalted musical talent; no such comfort brightened the bleakness for him. In spite of all this he must, as a man who approached the problems of practical life with soberness, have examined the chances of his enterprise. And he was also a God-fearing man whose art was dedicated to the Lord. Would not his humble piety admonish him that, in a world which already tended to different forms of religious observance, his clinging to styles and techniques of the past was, after all, nothing but a sign of un-Christian arrogance? And if he stubbornly tried to ignore this question, could he hope to convince others with the kind of music he so insistently maintained?

If we call that man a hero who triumphs over overwhelming odds, who, seeing all his efforts

leading to futility, gives his lifeblood for a noble cause, here we behold him. I spoke mock-
ingly of the knight of chivalry—that is not
what I mean now. Nor do I mean the reckless
solving of tactical difficulties, or enduring of
them, by those whom we regard and justly
praise as heroes in the accepted sense of the
word. I mean those heroes of far-reaching and
long-planned strategy whose accomplishments
men may recognize long after if at all: those
who, in full awareness of the consequences,
undergo deadly scientific experiments for the
benefit of mankind; explorers with the cer-
tainty of personal failure; inventors who know
that their own discoveries will kill them and
bring them neither thanks nor acknowledgment. Had Bach not been of this kind, our
world today would be the poorer by one of the
most astounding intellectual achievements of
man.

Let us observe yet another aspect of this
private, inconspicuous, even hidden heroism,
revealed in its subtlety only to the most sympa-
thetic penetration.

To this end we may take an analytical glance
at Bach's accomplishments during the last ten
years of his life, the time between 1740 and

1750. He carries on his teaching obligations; there are no more controversies with his superiors, but no extra efforts on his part either. He makes frequent short trips into the country, but the one journey of significance is that to Potsdam and Berlin in 1747. In his creative work a peculiar change can be observed. The man who in six years in Cöthen and the first ten in Leipzig produced such an astonishing amount of music that it seems almost impossible he could conceive and write it in so short a period—his tempo of production slows down.

In those sixteen fruitful years he wrote most of the pieces that are widely known: about one hundred and seventy church cantatas, the Passions, the Magnificat, all his chamber and orchestra music, three parts of the Klavierübung, one-half of the Well-tempered Clavier and all the other significant clavier works, the motets, most of the secular cantatas, and some of the most important works for organ. And in the following years no decrease in this bee-like industry can be seen. What remains for the last ten years? A few of the cantatas, the Goldberg Variations, the second part of the Well-tempered Clavier, the artistically less important Peasant Cantata; of organ works the variations on "Vom Himmel hoch," the six Schübler chorale preludes and the eighteen others, and finally the Musical Offering and the Art of Fugue. This means that the average production during the last ten years was hardly more than one opus a year. True, some of these works like the Art of Fugue, the chorale preludes, and the Well-tempered Clavier consist of numerous single pieces. Because of this and the intellectual effort involved in their composition they required considerable time to complete. But there are others, like the cantatas and variations, each of which the composer, with his often-shown dexterity, probably wrote in not more than a few days.

What is the reason for so sudden a decline? Certainly no senile withering of his productive energy. At his death in 1750 he had merely reached the age which nowadays sends a schoolteacher in a corresponding position into retirement. In 1740 he could expect ten or fifteen more working years. He was still vigorous enough, too, and the compositions written in those years show, if not in number at least in their spiritual and technical aspects, the fullest energy of his former periods of work. He who throughout his life had written *ad majorem*

Dei gloriam cannot suddenly have abandoned his sacred duty in a disloyal inertia. Had he lost his self-reliance, his belief in his musical talents? That cannot be the explanation either; such steadfast creations as the second part of the Well-tempered Clavier and the chorale preludes could only have been written with complete artistic equilibrium. Moreover, there is no sign of doubt of his capacity to surmount technical obstacles.

From now on a shadow seems to have fallen upon his creativeness, the shadow of melancholy. With reference to Brahms' compositions someone coined the malicious term "melancholy of artistic impotence." In Bach's case no incapacity, no artistic impotence is present. On the contrary, some compositions of his last ten years display a skill masterly to a degree never achieved before, either by himself or by others. Yet since the melancholic mood is undeniable, we are justified in calling it the melancholy of capacity, of artistic potency—and with this I believe we have found the answer to the riddle.

It is hard for us to think of reasons which could have caused a Bach at the top of his creative powers, in the fullest possession of his craft, to become the victim of a melancholic decline.

39

To understand it we must try to put ourselves in his place. What can a man do who technically and spiritually has climbed to the highest rung of artistic production attainable by mankind? He can climb no higher for he is only a man. Is he serenely to continue his former work, forcing it by mere rearrangement into apparently new forms? In the course of his ascent he has acquired such a sense of responsibility that this sort of thing must seem to him nothing but primitive reiteration and squandering. Why should he not simply relax now, and enjoy what he has achieved? He had never known idleness, he was born without such knowledge and never acquired it. Should he not work for the benefit of others, adapting his mature production to broader musical demands by changing its shape and purpose? The goal of his work, the direction of its effect, the mark his music leaves on the souls of others—all these have become nonessential accessories, which merely cover the creative activity loosely like a cape. This activity proper is now as independent of all those factors as is the sun of the life called forth by its rays—so independent that finally even realization in a work of art is not needed as proof of its existence. It has become pure thought, freed from all incidents and frailties of structural manifestation, and he who ascended relentlessly has defeated the realm of substance and penetrated the unlimited region of thought. But do we not, in perceiving this region as a goal, disavow all art? For to us who were denied the sublime ascent structures formed by creative thought are precisely what we recognize as art, that agent without whose admixture, be it even in minutest doses, our life would not be worth living, would even be impossible. The answer to this question has been left far behind by him who attained all that is humanly possible. He has arrived at the end, he stands, as the old Persian poem says, before the curtain that nobody will ever draw aside.

For this ultimate attainment he must pay a dear price: melancholy, the grief at having been bereft of all former imperfections and with them of the possibility of proceeding further. Perhaps on this extramundane plane of final bewilderment a sublimated repetition occurs of that exit-less situation which we are accustomed to illustrate with the figure of the scorpion that kills itself inside the circle of fire. There are men, too, who resort to suicide for fear of the descent into the unknown, into nothingness—as though this step would turn nought into something, the unknown into knowledge. This way out is barred for him who has climbed to the summit. Only one move is open to him: to apply the means he is wont to use in serenely enhancing, serenely adorning his steepest, narrowest, humblest abode on the outermost plateau. With this his creative work turns into sublime creativity, his craftsman's proficiency into philosophic vision.

Recognition of human excellence in its highest form, knowledge of the path that leads to it, the necessary done with dutifulness and driven to that point of perfection where it outgrows all necessity—this knowledge is the most precious inheritance given us with Bach's music.

What is our obligation toward this recognition? The specific obligation of the composer, as well as of the musician in general, we will merely touch on, because he is no uncommon case, although in practicing his craft he seems to move closer to our ideal, and there is no possibility of any musical aim with a higher ethical obligation existing for him than to follow Bach. To be resolved to seek the same road to perfection, more than that no one can do. He may proceed some stumbling paces, or fate may permit him to press far ahead. But whatever the measure and kind of his progression, he need not imitate the sounding structure of Bach's music. Questions of style, Bach's or anyone else's, under these aspects lose all meaning. So does concern with the externals of music, with beauty and ugliness, weight and lightness, with the Apollonian and the Dionysian. Even the search for comparative values of past and contemporary music, which nowadays seem so important to us, is superfluous then. One single type of music will emerge: music which in the sense of Bach's musical ethos, his most valuable bequest, is *right*.

The rest of us too, the nonmusicians, will have no difficulty in seeing the obligation that arises from this heritage. We have beheld the summit of musical greatness, a summit which has not been clouded through interference of the human, personal, time-conditioned, in short the profane problems of the composer's personality. This summit is, as we know, unattainable to us, but since we have beheld it we must not lose it from sight. It must always serve us as a supreme beacon. Like all other artistic issues this summit is a symbol, a symbol for everything noble toward which we strive with the better part of our being.

In the limited realm of musical enjoyment, which, in spite of its own beauty, is again a symbol of our whole faculty of perceiving and digesting earthly experiences, recognition of the summit, once and forever, means that from now on we cannot perceive any structure of sound without measuring it against those values which Bach has demonstrated. The outward hull of music, sound, will then shrink to nothingness. If originally it was the element which drew us toward music, which alone seemed to satisfy our longings, it is now only a vessel for something more important: our own betterment. Such betterment will make us intolerant of lesser music, idle tinkling, uncontrolled and unskilled composition. But it will also open our minds to music using symbols that are yet unknown to us, wrapped in strange sounds that we must first learn to decipher.

If music has the power to direct our entire existence toward nobleness, this music is great. If a composer has dominated his music to this point of greatness, he has achieved the utmost.

This Bach has achieved.